OUR KANSAS HOME

HOME

✱ Book Three ✱ of the Prairie Skies Series

DEBORAH HOPKINSON

✱

Illustrated by PATRICK FARICY

ALADDIN PAPERBACKS

New York   London   Toronto   Sydney   Singapore

This book is a work of fiction. Any references to historical events, real people, or real locales are used fictitiously. Other names, characters, places, and incidents are the product of the author's imagination, and any resemblance to actual events or locales or persons, living or dead, is entirely coincidental.

First Aladdin Paperbacks edition February 2003

Text copyright © 2003 by Deborah Hopkinson
Illustrations copyright © 2003 by Patrick Faricy

ALADDIN PAPERBACKS
An imprint of Simon & Schuster
Children's Publishing Division
1230 Avenue of the Americas
New York, NY 10020

Also available in an Aladdin Library edition.
Designed by Debra Sfetsios
The text of this book was set in ITC Century Book.

Printed in the United States of America
2 4 6 8 10 9 7 5 3 1

Library of Congress Control Number 2002113774

ISBN 0-689-84353-4

Ho, brothers! Come, brothers!
Hasten all with me.
We'll sing upon the Kansas plains,
A song of liberty.

from "Call to Kansas"

—Lucy Larcom

✳

ACKNOWLEDGMENTS

In researching *Our Kansas Home* I feel fortunate to have had online access to many original manuscripts, letters, and books written by Kansas citizens in the 1850s. This would not have been possible without the efforts of volunteers, who took the time to scan these documents and make them available online through the Kansas Collection (www.kancoll.org).

Thanks also to Kansas historian Paul Stuewe, who read the manuscript and offered many helpful suggestions. Thanks as well to the librarians of the Kansas State Historical Society and the interlibrary loan staff of Whitman College for their assistance, to Michele Hill for help with research in Kansas, and to Deborah Wiles for her insightful comments. I am also grateful to my editor, Ellen Krieger, for her encouragement. Any errors are mine.

For Toni and Jeremy

✳

OUR KANSAS
HOME

CHAPTER
ONE

Charlie Keller ran down the muddy road clutching two crinkled dollar bills in his hand.

"Calico, ribbon, and candy for Sadie," Charlie sang to himself. He didn't want to forget anything. "Calico, ribbon, and candy for Sadie.

"I promised Papa we'd meet him in ten minutes, Lion," Charlie told the golden dog trotting at his side. "So stay close."

Lion barked and flashed his big dog grin.

Charlie laughed. Finding Lion was the best thing that had happened to him since moving to Kansas. There was only one problem: Lion liked to wander.

"It's dangerous for Lion to roam the prairie," Papa had warned last fall, after Lion had run off for two days. "Besides, a dog costs money to feed. If we're going to keep Lion, he has to stick close and learn to be a watch-dog."

Ida Jane had chimed in. "You're nine now, Charlie. You and Lion just can't wander around looking at birds and plants all day. You have to train him."

Bossy Ida Jane! But Charlie knew his older sister was right, and so Charlie had worked hard with Lion all winter. Now Lion could sit, stay, and come when called.

At least Lion could do all these things at home. But would Lion obey Charlie in the busy town of Lawrence?

Charlie stopped outside the store. Time for Lion's first test.

"Stay," Charlie commanded. Lion's bright brown eyes sparkled. He wagged his tail, back and forth, back and forth. Then he plopped down. Perfect.

"Good dog. I'll be right back." Charlie patted Lion's head, turned, and—*bam!* He bumped right into a man with a long, sad face.

"Oh, sorry, Mr. Dillon," said Charlie. Sometimes people called Ed Dillon "Wooden Ed." He had a shop in town where he built wooden chairs and tables.

"Why, Charlie Keller of Spring Creek! Where's your pa?" asked Ed.

"Papa's buying cornmeal, molasses, and . . . ," Charlie began.

Wooden Ed held up his hand. "Hold on. Haven't you heard? The town's in danger. Sheriff Samuel Jones and his border ruffians are set to attack the Free State Hotel this very afternoon."

Charlie's eyes widened. "Sheriff Jones and his border ruffians!"

Charlie knew the border ruffians were rough men, willing to fight to make Kansas a slave state someday. But Charlie's family, and most people in Lawrence, wanted Kansas Territory to enter the Union as a free state, where owning slaves wouldn't be allowed.

"The whole country is watching Kansas," Papa had told Charlie. "If proslavery folks win here, slavery is sure to spread into other new territories in the West."

And the proslavery side was winning. Last year some proslavery men from Missouri had pretended to live in Kansas, so they could vote in the Kansas election. And they had won. That's why Kansas Territory had proslavery men like Sheriff Jones in charge.

Papa was still angry about the "bogus" election. "It wasn't fair," he told Charlie. "But now we're expected to

obey their laws and men like that rascal Jones. Why, Jones doesn't even live here; he's from Missouri!"

And if Sheriff Jones was in Lawrence with his gang of border ruffians, it could mean only one thing: trouble.

Wooden Ed strode off toward the hotel, pulling Charlie behind him.

"Wait, I almost forgot!" cried Charlie. "My dog."

Charlie whistled. In a flash Lion was at his side.

"Now, that's a well-trained pup you've got," said Ed.

"Lion's a good boy," Charlie said proudly, patting Lion on the head.

"I guess your pa's been too busy on his farm to keep up with the news in town," Ed said as they rushed toward the hotel.

Charlie nodded. "Pa planted six acres of corn. Momma says if we don't get a good crop, she has a mind to go back to Massachusetts. She claims she couldn't live through another winter like this past one."

"It *was* rough on all the new settlers," Ed agreed.

What a winter! The prairie wind had never stopped whistling and moaning. Most mornings their drinking water had been frozen solid in the pail. Little Sadie, who was just five, had been sick a lot.

And once, Charlie had found Momma crying softly as she rocked Baby Henry.

"We came here to find a new life, and to keep the evil of slavery from spreading," Momma had whispered, tears in her eyes. "But I never dreamed life would be so hard."

At least it's spring now, thought Charlie. The May sun felt warm on his back. But he couldn't help worrying about what might happen next.

If the border ruffians made trouble all summer, Papa and the other settlers wouldn't have time to work on their new farms. If they didn't grow enough food, some families might give up and go back to their home states. Just what the border ruffians wanted!

I wonder if we'll *go back*, Charlie thought.

Charlie hadn't wanted to leave Massachusetts. He still missed Grandpa and his old dog, Danny. Sometimes, if he closed his eyes, he could almost imagine himself hunting bird nests in their old woods and catching polliwogs in the pond.

Still, Charlie was growing to like Kansas. He loved the way hawks soared in the big prairie skies.

Charlie liked the people he'd met, too. Especially his friend, Flory Morgan. Flory always made him smile. She called him "Massachusetts Charlie," and sang old river songs in her high, sweet voice.

The truth was Charlie didn't know where he belonged anymore.

Massachusetts or Kansas. Which was home now?

CHAPTER
TWO

"There's the Free State Hotel!" cried Charlie. "I think it must be the grandest building in Kansas."

"Now families have a fine place to stay when they arrive," Ed said proudly. "But Sheriff Jones and the proslavery folks claim it's a fort. They say we free-state settlers might use it to overthrow the government."

A crowd of men had gathered in front of the hotel. Charlie stood on tiptoes to look for Papa.

Wooden Ed squinted. "Can you spot him?"

"No. Oh, wait. There he is. Papa!" Charlie hollered. A tall, thin man with dark hair shouldered his way toward them.

"Good to see you, Ed," said Papa, shaking Mr. Dillon's hand. "So it looks like more trouble."

Ed nodded. "Sheriff Jones has been coming around for weeks, trying to arrest the free-state leaders. Especially anyone who helped rescue Jacob Branson."

He gave Papa a long look and added, "They haven't noticed me. Yet . . ."

Charlie felt a wave of fear rush over him. Last fall Sheriff Jones had arrested a free-state man named Jacob Branson for no good reason. Some of Branson's friends had rescued him because they feared the sheriff might hurt him.

Charlie would never forget that night. He had hidden in the wagon. But Papa and Ed Dillon had stood up with the other free-state men.

Will Sheriff Jones go after Papa, too? Charlie wondered.

"It didn't help that some fool shot at Jones a few weeks ago," Ed went on.

"Now, that was wrong," said Papa. "Is Jones all right?"

"He was wounded, but he's better," Ed replied. "And madder than ever. He wants to punish the whole town. And destroying the hotel is one way to do it."

Just then a man rode up and stopped his horse right in front of them. "They're coming!" he shouted. "Jones and his men are riding down from the top of Mount Oread."

At that moment the man's horse reared. Its hooves

9

came down near Charlie and Lion. Papa grabbed Charlie, and pulled him to safety.

Lion yelped. Charlie made a grab for him, but Lion was spooked. He started to run, tail between his legs.

"Lion!" Charlie yelled. "Oh, I have to catch him."

Before Papa could stop him, Charlie pushed his way through the crowd of men.

At the corner he stopped. He didn't see Lion anywhere.

It wasn't Lion's fault, thought Charlie. *He couldn't help being scared.*

"Lion! Here, boy!" Charlie yelled.

He turned the corner and froze in horror.

"Border ruffians," he whispered.

I should run, thought Charlie. But he couldn't make his feet move.

He was standing in front of the newspaper office. Charlie could read the sign: KANSAS FREE STATE. As he watched, four or five men smashed the door open.

They rushed inside, whooping and shouting. Charlie heard loud crashes and bangs.

Suddenly a chair came flying out the door. Charlie jumped back.

Then came a desk, and another chair.

Someone threw out a lantern. *Crash!* The glass broke into a hundred pieces.

Next came equipment, stacks of paper, and old newspapers.

A man came up behind Charlie. "They're wrecking the printing press. They won't stop until the newspaper office is destroyed."

A shower of black metal poured out the door. Some of the bits landed at Charlie's feet. He bent down and picked one of them up. He turned the small piece of metal over in his hand.

"What is it?" Charlie asked the man.

"That's a piece of type. It's a letter the printer uses to set a page of print," the man told him. "Won't be much good now."

Then the man walked away, his shoulders slumped.

Charlie peered at the tiny object in his hand. It was the capital letter "L."

"Words have power," Momma had told him, when he first learned to read. Charlie hadn't understood what she meant. Now Charlie thought he knew.

These men didn't want anyone writing about making Kansas a free state. They didn't want people to speak out against slavery. They didn't want anything to change.

One of the men came out of the building and pointed at Charlie. "Hey, boy, what you lookin' at?"

In a flash Charlie slipped the tiny letter into his pocket. He spun on his heel and ran hard.

"Lion. Here, boy," Charlie called as he ran.

Charlie wanted to find Lion more than ever. He felt scared to be walking alone.

He called again.

All at once he heard a bark. Lion came running toward him.

Lion leaned against Charlie's leg and pushed his wet nose against Charlie's hand. He plopped to the ground and rolled over to have his belly scratched.

It wasn't my fault that big horse scared me, Lion seemed to be saying.

Charlie couldn't help smiling. "Come on, Lion."

"There you are," said Papa as Charlie slipped in beside him. "Hold Lion close, now."

Charlie heard shouts and the pounding of hooves.

"They're here," said Ed grimly.

CHAPTER
THREE

"Kansas is ours!"

"Let's see how strong the Free State Hotel really is!"

"Get rid of this fort! Down with treason!"

The shouts of the Missouri men filled the air. Charlie craned his neck. Everywhere he looked he saw men on horseback, bearing down on the hotel.

He whispered to Papa, "There are so many."

"Maybe eight hundred," said Papa. "But don't worry, Charlie. They're after buildings, not people."

Ed nodded. "Everyone in the hotel got out safely."

"But can't we stop them? Can't we do *something*?" Charlie cried.

"Not this time," Ed said, laying his hand on Charlie's shoulder. "Jones is still angry that we defied him last fall, when we rescued Branson. Now he has eight hundred men with him. And the proslavery government is on his side."

"But . . . but . . . we can't just stand here!" Charlie said.

Papa looked at Ed Dillon, but Ed shook his head. "The townspeople talked about it. In the end we figured that if we fought back, Jones would use it as an excuse to burn down the whole town."

As Charlie watched, the border ruffians pointed a cannon straight at the Free State Hotel.

"But the hotel is made of stone," Charlie said. "They won't be able to hurt it, will they?"

Papa put his arm around Charlie's shoulder. He didn't say a word.

Boom! The cannonball flew clear over the roof of the hotel. The townspeople cheered.

Lion began to whine. The hair on his neck stood straight up. Charlie held him tight. "It's all right, boy."

Boom! The cannon fired again. This time the cannonball hit the hotel, but the walls didn't crumble.

"Hurrah!" shouted the townspeople.

Charlie felt like jumping up and down. "It's too strong, Papa. They can't wreck it."

"I hope you're right, Charlie."

Sheriff Jones ordered his men to explode a keg of gunpowder inside the hotel.

Crack! Bang! The air filled with smoke. The hotel still stood. The townspeople cheered once more.

"Maybe he'll give up now," said Charlie.

"I'm afraid not," said Wooden Ed, pointing. "Look, they're trying to burn it down."

Papa sighed. "Once the mattresses and beds catch fire, the floors will go."

Charlie looked around him. The townspeople had stopped cheering. Slowly the smell of smoke seeped into the air. Soon Charlie heard a crackling sound coming from inside the hotel. Clouds of smoke billowed overhead.

Now it was the border ruffians' turn to cheer and shout. The people of Lawrence knew it was too dangerous to fight Sheriff Jones and his men. Still, it was hard to watch. Charlie saw Papa clenching his fists. Ed Dillon bit his lip so hard it started to bleed.

Sheriff Jones began to laugh. Charlie heard him say, "I can make these free-state men bow before me in the dust and kiss the laws of Kansas Territory! Come on, men. Let's go."

As the border ruffians were about to leave, one of them wheeled his horse close to Charlie. He pointed at

Papa and Ed Dillon. "Hold on a minute. You two look familiar. Weren't you part of that group of traitors who stole our prisoner last fall?"

Charlie felt ready to burst. Without thinking, he shouted, "Jacob Branson wasn't stolen. He was *rescued!*"

"That's enough, Charlie. Hush." Papa placed a strong hand on Charlie's shoulder.

The man shook his rifle at Papa and Ed. "Well, if you were there that night, you're lucky you haven't been arrested yet. Watch out!"

He spurred his horse, and galloped off.

Charlie swallowed hard. "Will that man have you arrested, Papa?"

"I don't think so, Charlie." Papa said softly. "We're not well-known leaders like the others."

Ed Dillon chewed his lip. "That's so. But maybe we *should* lie low for a few days. My sister has a place out of the way, twenty miles north of town."

Papa shook his head. "Ed, I can't leave my claim, especially now. Sarah would be alone with four children, including a baby."

"Your wife would want you to be safe, James," insisted Ed.

Charlie looked from Mr. Dillon to Papa. Suddenly Charlie knew what he had to say.

"Papa, go with Mr. Dillon, please," he pleaded. "You can't take a chance. You must hide!"

CHAPTER
FOUR

"I'm ready, Papa," said Charlie.

It was late afternoon. The Free State Hotel was a charred shell. The border ruffians had smashed both newspaper presses. They had stolen food and horses. And they'd burned down the home of Charles Robinson, one of the town's leaders.

"Don't worry, Papa. Remember, Lion and I have gone home alone before," Charlie said. "It's only a few miles."

Papa hesitated. "It's more dangerous now."

"It might be dangerous on the road. That's why I won't take the wagon. Lion and I will hide in the grass if we see anyone. I won't have anything the border ruffians can steal," said Charlie.

Charlie drew himself up as tall as he could, and looked into Papa's eyes. "Papa, I can do this. Besides, Lion will warn me if anyone comes near."

Lion barked once.

20

"Your boy's growing up, James," Ed said to Papa.

"I shouldn't have brought you with me, Charlie," Papa said with a sigh. "You're only nine."

Wooden Ed slapped his knee and laughed. "What do you mean, *only* nine? Why, nine is pretty near grown around these parts. Charlie's got a good head on his shoulders. Besides, he's got the fiercest-lookin' guard dog west of the Mississippi!"

At the moment Lion didn't look fierce at all. In fact he was scratching his ear with his hind leg. Charlie couldn't help smiling.

I do have a good head on my shoulders, Charlie told himself. *I can do this.*

"Tell Momma I'll be home as soon as I can," Papa said.

Charlie reached into his pocket and handed Papa the two dollars. As he did, his fingers touched the tiny piece of metal.

"I never got Sadie that stick of candy she wanted," said Charlie.

"Someday I hope Lawrence will be safe enough that Sadie can come and choose her own candy," Papa replied.

He patted Charlie's arm. "Be careful, Charlie."

"I'm sure the border ruffians have all headed back to Franklin to celebrate their victory," Ed Dillon added. "Believe me, all they'll be thinking about tonight is whiskey."

Franklin! Charlie frowned. "Papa, my friend Flory lives in Franklin. Will she and her father be safe?"

Flory and her father were from Missouri. But Flory's father wasn't like the border ruffians. Mr. Morgan believed the future of Kansas should be decided by voting, not by fighting.

"Don't worry about Flory and her father, Charlie," Papa told him. "The border ruffians won't bother them."

As he hugged his father good-bye, Charlie hoped Papa was right.

Swish, swish. Swish, swish.

Charlie pushed his way through the prairie grass; he could recognize different kinds now: big bluestem and little bluestem, wild rye, switchgrass, and sharp-edged cordgrass. Soon the grass would be taller than he was.

Charlie stopped and looked across the prairie. Most days it took his breath away. The grass waved, and ribbons of wildflowers fluttered.

He longed to go exploring. He wanted to send wild-flowers pressed in a letter to Grandpa. Grandpa would love bluets and prairie violets, sundrops and prim-roses.

But I can't look at flowers today, Charlie thought. Instead he made himself be as alert as a deer. He watched the road, ready to pounce into the brush and hide if anyone appeared.

I used to roam and dream for hours, Charlie thought. *But now I've learned to keep my wits about me.*

"We're safe so far," Charlie said to Lion. "Maybe Wooden Ed was right. The border ruffians must have all gone back to their camp."

The sun began to sink, turning the sky a deep rose. It would be dark soon. Charlie walked faster. He didn't want to take a chance of being lost at night on the prairie.

Suddenly Lion shot out ahead.

"Lion, come back!" Charlie ran to catch up.

Lion planted his feet in front of some low bushes and began to whine softly.

Something is in there, Charlie realized. But what? It might be a rabbit or a prairie chicken. Or even a rattle-snake.

Charlie tried to grab Lion to pull him back. But Lion wouldn't budge. He whined again.

Slowly, slowly, Charlie leaned down. He pushed away a branch and peered into the bushes.

A pair of eyes stared straight back at him.

CHAPTER
FIVE

Charlie jumped back, startled.

Lion barked. The person drew back into the bushes, cringing in fear. Charlie took a breath. He bent down and looked again.

It was a young woman, a girl, really. A girl with dark skin.

At first Charlie felt confused. Who was she? Why was she hiding?

Charlie gulped. He leaned forward and whispered, "Um . . . hello. I'm Charlie. Charlie Keller."

No answer.

Lion whined. He sniffed at the girl's legs. She gasped and drew back farther.

Charlie noticed that the girl's feet were bare. Her legs were covered with scratches and bites.

And then all at once Charlie understood.

A runaway! The girl was a runaway slave!

Charlie grabbed hold of Lion. "He's friendly. He won't hurt you."

The girl stared back at him. Charlie thought that at any minute she would spring up and run away. He kept talking.

"I'm hiding, too, in a way," Charlie told her. "I don't want to meet any border ruffians on the road. On account of my family are free-soilers."

Charlie paused. "You can trust me, miss."

The young girl in the bushes didn't take her eyes off Charlie and Lion. At last she said softly, "I'm heading for a town called Lawrence. But there've been all sorts of men ridin' up and down the road."

Her voice surprised Charlie. It had a soft, sweet rhythm, like water flowing over stones.

"Those are the border ruffians," Charlie told her. "They've gone back to their camp now, I think. But there was bad trouble in Lawrence today.

"You could come with me," he offered. "To our cabin at Spring Creek. We can get there by walking across the fields. You would be safe there. My momma will know what to do."

27

Charlie hoped that this was true. He had heard Papa and Momma talk about folks in Lawrence hiding runaway slaves. But would Momma be willing to hide this girl?

The girl looked doubtful. "You sure?"

Charlie nodded. He waited. Would she decide to trust him?

Slowly the girl crawled out from under the bushes. She was very thin, with warm brown skin. Her dress was a faded green. She carried a small bundle tied up in a blue cloth.

Lion came close to sniff her. The girl backed away. Lion plopped down and rolled on his back. He pawed the air, begging to have his belly scratched.

"He likes you. He's a nice dog," Charlie assured her.

The girl shook her head. "I don't like dogs."

Then she looked at Charlie and said, "I'm Lizzie. I want to go to Canada."

Lion went first, then Charlie. Lizzie followed behind. Charlie kept turning to make sure she was there. He was afraid she might turn around and run into the darkness. Or maybe her feet hurt and she was just tired and hungry.

By the time they reached the cabin, the stars were out, thousands of them in clusters like prairie wildflowers.

At the cabin door, Charlie glanced back at the girl.

"Come in. It's all right," he whispered.

Lizzie stepped back into the darkness. "I'll wait. If it's safe, you come back."

Charlie opened the door.

"Momma," he said softly.

Momma was nursing Baby Henry in their one good chair, a wooden rocker that Ed Dillon had made.

Instantly she jumped up. "What's kept you and Papa? I must have dozed off. I didn't hear the wagon."

Sadie and Ida Jane were already asleep on their mattress of prairie hay. But when the door opened, Ida Jane sat up and rubbed her eyes.

Charlie wasn't sure what to tell first. "Momma, I'm not alone. Someone is here. She needs our help."

Then Charlie stepped out and drew Lizzie inside.

Lizzie blinked in the lantern light. Momma rose up out of her chair, shifted the sleeping baby to her shoulder, and walked toward them.

"Charlie, where is Papa? Is he all right?" she whispered in a frightened voice. "And who is this?"

Charlie rushed to explain. "Papa's fine. But the border ruffians attacked Lawrence today. They burned the Free State Hotel. They smashed the newspaper office, too. I saw it myself."

Charlie stopped for a breath. "One of the border ruffians recognized Papa and Mr. Dillon. They've been arresting all the free-state leaders. So Mr. Dillon thought he and Papa should hide for a few days."

Ida Jane bounded out of bed and stood next to Momma. "What did you do then, Charlie? Was it awfully exciting?"

Ida Jane looked at Lizzie. "I'm Ida Jane. I'm eleven, the oldest. Who are you?"

"Hush, Ida Jane," ordered Momma. "Go on, Charlie. Tell it in your own time."

"Well, Papa and Mr. Dillon took our wagon and went to stay at Mr. Dillon's sister's farm. Papa was afraid the border ruffians might steal the wagon and the supplies if I drove it home," Charlie explained.

Momma turned toward the stranger. "And what is your name?"

"Lizzie, ma'am."

"Lizzie was trying to get to Lawrence," Charlie put in. "But there were too many border ruffians riding up and down the road."

"I see," said Momma. She fell silent, frowning.

Charlie waited, holding his breath. *Momma understands Lizzie is a runaway*, he thought. But what would Momma do? Would she let Lizzie stay?

"I've heard some folks in Lawrence are active in the underground railroad, helping runaways get north to Canada," said Momma. "Back in Massachusetts, it was easy to be brave," she went on, shifting the baby on her shoulder. "Here we could go to jail for taking in a runaway slave."

Momma moved closer and put out her hand to Lizzie. "But there is only one thing to do. Lizzie, you must stay. Whatever happens, we will help you the best we can."

Charlie let out his breath at last.

At that moment Sadie sat up in bed and looked around.

"Charlie," she said in an accusing voice. "You forgot my candy, didn't you?"

CHAPTER
SIX

"That was delicious. Thank you, ma'am," said Lizzie, mopping up the last bite of rabbit stew with a biscuit.

Charlie nodded. "It tasted wonderful, Momma."

"I kept it warm, since I was expecting you and Papa," Momma said with a sigh. She had put Baby Henry to bed and bustled to feed Lizzie and Charlie. Ida Jane had warmed some water so Lizzie could soak the blisters on her feet.

"Lizzie, tomorrow we'll get word to our neighbors, the Engles. They may be able to help you get to Canada," said Momma.

"What if someone comes looking for Lizzie?" asked Ida Jane. "What will we do then?"

"You're right, Ida Jane. We need a plan." Momma thought a minute. "Here's what we'll do. I will take to my bed with the chills. I'll have Baby Henry bundled beside me, and every blanket and quilt we own piled on the bed."

Charlie was puzzled. "I don't understand, Momma."

But Ida Jane clapped her hands. "Lizzie can be hiding under the covers. The way Sadie likes to snuggle up with Momma on a cold morning."

Momma nodded. "That's the idea. No man would dare disturb a sick mother and a baby." She turned to Lizzie. "Would you be willing to hide in the bed if someone comes?"

Lizzie nodded. She smiled for the first time. "It will be easy for me, ma'am. I'm skinny as a rail."

"Now repeat what I told you, Charlie," ordered Momma early the next morning, as she fried eggs and potatoes, and set a pan of biscuits to bake.

"If anyone stops us, we tell them our papa is away and our mother is sick with fever," Charlie said. He knew no one would question that. Lots of people in Kansas had the fever.

Ida Jane tied on her bonnet. "Then we tell them we're headed to our neighbors to get help. But we're *really* going to ask Mr. Engle if he knows anyone who can help Lizzie get to Canada."

Sadie took a bite of egg. She frowned and chewed slowly. "Momma, are you sick with the fever?"

"Oh, no, Sadie Sunshine," said Momma, patting Sadie's curls. "But we do need our neighbors' help."

Charlie and Ida Jane glanced at each other. Sadie was only five. Could she understand how important it was to keep quiet about Lizzie, if anyone came to the door?

Charlie thought Momma must have been worried about the same thing, for Momma leaned over and put her hands on Sadie's shoulders.

"Sadie, if anyone does come, you must be as still as a mouse, no matter what happens," Momma said sternly. "This is very important. You must not tell anyone Lizzie is here, or that you have ever seen her. Lizzie's life could depend on it. Do you understand?"

Sadie nodded and looked at Lizzie. Her lip trembled and she whispered, "I promise, Momma."

Then Sadie buried her face in Momma's dress and began to cry.

Charlie was glad to have Ida Jane's company on the walk, especially since Momma wanted to keep Lion at home.

"Lion will be our watchdog. He'll warn us if anyone comes," Momma had said.

Charlie stood in front of his dog and spoke firmly. "Momma is depending on you, Lion."

Lion seemed to understand. He sat straight without moving, and watched Charlie and Ida Jane walk away. Charlie looked back at him proudly.

"I hope I get to ride in a wagon at night and help Lizzie escape," Ida Jane said as the cabin disappeared from view. "All the exciting things have been happening to you, Charlie. I want something to happen to me, too."

Charlie pointed. "Maybe it will. Look, someone's riding toward us."

Ida Jane squinted in the sun. "It's only Mr. Engle."

"Ida Jane! Charlie! Where's your father?" called Mr. Engle, pulling up his horse.

"Papa's away. He's hiding so the border ruffians won't arrest him," Ida Jane told him.

Mr. Engle spoke quickly. "Run back and warn your mother. I hear border ruffians may be headed this way. They've been roaming the countryside since dawn, stealing every chicken and cow they can get their hands on."

Mr. Engle turned his horse's head. "Try to hide your stock. I've got to get home and do the same."

Ida Jane stretched out her hand. "Wait, Mr. Engle! We were coming to see you. We have . . . a friend at our house. A friend who wants to go to Canada."

"Until this business settles down, the 'railroad' won't be running," Mr. Engle told them, spurring his horse. "Do the best you can for now. Later in the summer we can help."

Chickens and cows, chickens and cows!

How can we get all the chickens and cows hidden? Charlie wondered. *And what about Lizzie?*

"Ida Jane," he gasped as their feet pounded the dirt. "Sadie and Momma have more than twenty baby chicks. And there's Annie and her calf. How can we hide them?"

Ida Jane's bonnet was tipped over one eye. Her long braids bounced on her shoulders as she ran. "Don't talk to me, I'm thinking!"

Charlie tried to come up with a plan, too. But all he could picture in his mind were the awful things he had seen in Lawrence: the smashed printing press and flames shooting from the Free State Hotel.

The cabin was still and quiet. *We're safe so far,* Charlie thought.

"Momma, Momma!" Ida Jane shouted as they came closer. "Mr. Engle says the border ruffians are coming! They're looking to steal chickens and cows. We need flour sacks."

Momma rushed out of the cabin with the baby in her arms. Her face was pale.

"I have an idea," Ida Jane gasped. "Sadie and I can scoop up some of the hens and chicks into flour sacks. We'll run to the woods near the creek, and hide in the blackberry thicket. They'll never find us in the thick brush."

Charlie stared at his sister. Chickens in flour sacks? What a crazy idea!

But Momma nodded. "Why not? Don't take them all, though. The men will suspect something if they see an empty coop."

Ida Jane ran for the sacks. "Come on, Sadie, you can help. We're going to save your favorite chickens."

"What about Annie?" asked Charlie. "How can we hide Annie and her calf?"

Momma froze. Annie was her prized possession.

Momma had been determined to get a cow so that they could have fresh milk and butter.

"Maybe I can take the cows and try to hide them down by the creek, too," Charlie offered.

Charlie ran to the stable. He managed to get a rope on Annie and her calf.

"I'll hide the milk pails. And I'll cover the ground with hay to hide any trace of them," said Lizzie, who had run in behind him to help. "You can say your pa is in town with the oxen. They might not guess you have cows, too."

Charlie nodded. "Good idea."

They were just coming out of the stable leading the cows when Lion leaped to his feet and began to bark. In the distance Charlie spotted a cloud of dust. "They're coming."

"Ida Jane. Run, now!" yelled Momma.

Squawk! Cheep! Cheep!
Squawk! Cheep! Cheep!

Ida Jane and Sadie disappeared into the high prairie grass, dragging two wriggling sacks of squawking chickens behind them.

Charlie felt his heart pounding hard. He looked from Momma to Lizzie. "What should we do? There's not enough time to get the cows to the creek."

"The most important thing is to hide Lizzie," cried Momma. "I'm afraid we can't save the cows."

"Wait, ma'am," said Lizzie. "Why not put the cows where no one will expect them to be?"

And then she told them her plan.

CHAPTER
SEVEN

Charlie held his tiny brother while Momma dragged her wooden rocking chair outside. She grabbed a quilt and the pan of leftover biscuits. She settled herself into the chair and reached up for the baby.

"It's lucky he's such a lazy baby," said Charlie. "He can sleep through anything."

Then Charlie and Lizzie went to work. They pulled Annie and her calf into the cabin. The cows looked so funny inside. Charlie had brought some hay for them, and they chewed peacefully.

"They think it's just a nice, new barn," Charlie said.

Charlie lifted the mattress of prairie hay from Momma's wooden bed and Lizzie got under it. Then he piled every quilt and blanket they had on top.

"Can you breathe, Lizzie?" he whispered.

"A little." Lizzie's voice sounded far away.

Charlie pulled Lion into a corner of the cabin, behind

his bed. He kept his hand on Lion's muzzle.

"Shh . . . you have to be perfectly still now," he whispered.

If I put my ear to the wall right here, I might be able to hear Momma talk to the men, Charlie thought.

Charlie closed his eyes and made his breath thin. He could feel little drops of sweat roll down his back.

A moment later he felt the ground rumble. He heard the pounding of hooves. A horse neighed. The silence was pierced by a man's wild yell.

The border ruffians were here.

Charlie could just barely make out Momma's voice.

"Good morning, gentlemen. Lovely day, isn't—"

A deep voice cut her off. "This is the Keller claim, ain't it? Where's your husband?"

"I wish I knew, sir. He went to Lawrence and hasn't come back." Momma paused, and Charlie could imagine her smiling brightly. "Now, gentlemen, I baked extra biscuits this morning. But since my husband's not here, you're welcome to them. And if I do say so myself, I make excellent biscuits!"

Charlie kept his hand on Lion's muzzle. Luckily Annie and her calf were still eating quietly.

"I've been sickly all winter, since my baby was born."

Momma chatted away in a loud voice. "I do believe this warm sun is the only thing that will keep me alive before I head back East."

Charlie heard footsteps running here and there. "There's nothing in the barn," one of the men yelled. "Where's your stock?"

Momma laughed, as if she didn't have a care in the world. "Oh, my husband took our oxen to town with him. All he's left with me is some tough, old chickens. You're welcome to them.

"He built that stable with dreams of being successful enough to own hogs, horses, and cows. But I'm afraid he's a poor farmer. Believe me, gentlemen, if I have any-thing to say about it, we will leave Kansas before the summer is over."

Momma's trying to convince the border ruffians we have nothing to steal, Charlie thought.

He heard a low murmur of voices.

"You want these chickens, or not?" one man called.

"Naw," said another. "The lady's right. They're tough old birds."

And then Charlie heard footsteps. Footsteps coming right to the door.

Lion heard the footsteps, too. He began wiggling in Charlie's arms. He struggled and gave a low whine. Charlie held him more tightly.

Momma's voice came again, loud and cheerful. "Sir, I wonder if you could get me a dipper of water from the pail by the door there? I would get up from my chair, but my legs are still weak. Are you by chance married with a babe of your own?"

A pause. Charlie tried with all his might to keep Lion quiet.

The man said, "Yes, ma'am. We have a little girl."

"Oh! Then you must worry about your loved ones when you leave them alone."

The footsteps started up again. But this time the man was walking away from the house.

"Thank you, sir. That water tastes good," Momma said.

Charlie heard the man call out, "Come on, boys. We're wasting our time here."

Then the man said something else to Momma in a low voice, but Charlie could not make out what it was.

Momma let a full twenty minutes pass after the men left before she called to Charlie. "It's safe now."

Charlie and Lizzie scrambled out of their hiding places. They opened the door and let Annie and her calf out.

Momma gave Charlie a big hug. Her eyes were wet with unshed tears.

Momma wiped her forehead with her white handkerchief. "Go and find Sadie and Ida Jane, Charlie."

But Sadie and Ida Jane were already coming over the hill. Sadie ran and buried her head in Momma's skirts.

Ida Jane let down her sacks of chickens. "We fooled them, didn't we? I knew we could do it!"

Lion was happy to be loose. He jumped up and down. He licked Charlie on the face and raced around, barking.

"Momma, what did that man say to you just before he left?" Charlie asked later.

"That man suspected I was play-acting," said Momma. "I was so frightened. I felt sure he would burst right through the door and find you.

"He looked me straight in the eye and said, 'Ma'am, I do believe you are hiding something—or someone. But I will spare you this time, for the sake of your baby. And perhaps someone will do the same for *my* wife and child.'"

47

CHAPTER
EIGHT

A few days later Papa slipped home on foot, under the cover of darkness.

Charlie thought Papa seemed worried. He went to the cabin door again and again, looking out.

"Lion keeps watch outside now," Charlie told him. "He'll bark if anyone comes."

But even with Lion as a watchdog, no one slept much. Charlie heard Momma and Papa talking late into the night.

"James, I fear for your life if you stay here at Spring Creek," Momma said softly. "If the border ruffians find you here, you'll be outnumbered."

Papa's voice was low and fierce. "Things *are* bad. It looks as if there will be fighting all summer. It's not only the proslavery men causing trouble now. A free-state man named John Brown has killed five of his proslavery neighbors."

"Then you must help protect Lawrence and help the free-state men," Momma whispered back. "And maybe you can try to arrange safe passage to Canada for Lizzie. We must not let her master find her."

Momma took a breath. "Don't worry about us. We will make do."

And they had.

Each morning they got up at five. Ida Jane and Charlie took turns milking Annie. Sadie was in charge of the chickens. Even though she was little, Sadie knew which hens made good mothers. She always managed to bring Momma fresh eggs each day.

But Charlie thought they might not have made it without Lizzie. Baby Henry was just six months old, and Momma still needed to nurse him.

"These few mouths are easy to cook for, compared to what I'm used to," Lizzie had told Momma. "Besides, it's a way of showing my thanks."

Lizzie was a good cook. She made delicious soups and stews with the meat, onions, carrots, and cabbage. Lizzie and Sadie scoured the land near the creek for dandelion greens, strawberries, and wild plums. And later, when it was hot, Lizzie cut up plums, sliced them, and spread them out in the sun to dry.

It seemed to Charlie that Lizzie knew a little about almost everything. She helped Charlie set traps for rabbits, quail, and prairie chicken. She knew about gardening, too, and helped tend the corn and the kitchen garden.

And at night, when they settled outside and rested, Lizzie sang. Her songs reminded Charlie of Flory. He hoped Flory was safe.

But then Charlie realized that none of them was really safe, not this summer.

There was danger everywhere.

One hot afternoon Charlie was fetching water when he heard a shout.

"Charlie, come quickly!" called Ida Jane.

Charlie shifted his shoulders carefully to balance the yoke better. Water was precious. He didn't want to spill even one drop in the two buckets he carried.

Trees edged Spring Creek like a border of lace. Charlie stepped out from under the shade into the high grass. The hot sun blazed down on his back.

The sky was a wide, brilliant blue. Charlie knew he'd be thirsty long before he reached the cabin.

At least Spring Creek is big enough so that we have water in the summer, Charlie thought. Momma had hoped for a well, so water would be close by. But with all the trouble this summer, Papa would not be able to dig a well this year.

"Charlie! Where are you?"

"Over here."

Ida Jane burst through the grass, her face red with the heat, her bonnet swinging over her shoulders. "A wagon's coming."

"Border ruffians?"

"Momma doesn't think so. They usually come on horses. But she sent Lizzie to hide."

Just then they heard Sadie's voice. "Charlie, Ida Jane, come quick! It's Flory!"

As soon as Charlie saw Flory next to the wagon, his heart sank. Carefully he placed his buckets on the ground. He came up slowly.

"Hello, Massachusetts Charlie," said Flory, without smiling.

Charlie pointed to the wagon, piled high with supplies. "You're leaving."

Flory nodded. "I begged my daddy to drive over here

to let you know. Last night some free-state men attacked the little fort at Franklin, near our house. Daddy says he feels caught between two worlds. He's afraid for us to stay."

Sadie came up and hung on Flory's dress. "Don't go, Flory. Live with us and teach us more songs about the Big Muddy."

"Things are sure to get better," Charlie said. "Papa says sooner or later the government in Washington, D.C., will have to do something to bring peace to Kansas."

Flory sighed. "This is for the best, Daddy says."

"But where will you go, Flory?" Ida Jane asked. "Are you headed back to Missouri?"

Flory glanced over at her father, who was saying good-bye to Momma.

Mr. Morgan shook his head. "No, we're going to start over somewhere new. We're heading farther west. I don't know where we'll end up. Maybe Santa Fe, maybe Texas. Who knows? We might even make it all the way to California."

Charlie swallowed. "We get our mail in Lawrence. If you write me, I promise to write back."

Flory flashed a smile. She leaned forward and

planted a kiss on Charlie's cheek. "That would be tremendously wonderful, Massachusetts Charlie."

Charlie waved until the wagon was out of sight.

If this trouble lasts much longer, we might be leaving, too, he thought.

CHAPTER
NINE

One hot night Charlie threw off his thin blanket and sat up. He rubbed his eyes.

He had been dreaming. He had been home in Massachusetts, walking through a field with old Danny. Had Danny barked in the dream?

"Woof!"

Suddenly Charlie was awake. He wasn't in Massachusetts at all. He was in their cabin at Spring Creek. It was the middle of the night. And Lion was barking.

Charlie jumped up and shook Momma. "Someone's coming."

"Lizzie! Come hide under the mattress. Quick," said Momma, instantly awake. "Ida Jane, throw your grandmother's quilt over me and light the lantern. Then dip a cloth in water and lay it on my forehead for my fever."

In an instant their cabin was transformed into a sickroom. Momma lay in bed, Baby Henry tucked beside her. Lizzie lay hidden under the mattress, trying not to move a muscle. Ida Jane sat by Momma's side, trying to look anxious.

"At least Sadie didn't wake up," whispered Momma. "She can't seem to understand that I'm not really sick! Now, Charlie, it's up to you. Go outside and keep Lion quiet so he doesn't get shot."

"Good luck, Charlie," said Ida Jane.

Charlie opened the cabin door. The voices of crickets filled the night.

"Lion, come!" Charlie called.

Instantly Lion trotted to his side and sat. Charlie commanded, "Be still, now."

Charlie looked up. The moon was a sliver of white. The black, starry sky seemed to stretch out forever.

It's up to me, he thought.

If border ruffians came now, there was nothing he could do to save Annie, her calf, or Sadie's chickens.

But he had to save Lizzie.

I'll have to convince the searchers that Momma is really sick, Charlie thought. He would have to make sure no one guessed they were hiding Lizzie.

Charlie remembered that winter day, long ago, when

Papa had first told them about moving to Kansas. Working to make Kansas a free state hadn't meant much, then.

But standing alone in the dark night, Charlie understood better why his father had wanted to come to Kansas.

"If Kansas is a free state someday, no one will have to hide," Charlie whispered to Lion.

Lion whined, but didn't bark. The sounds came closer. In the deep shadow a wagon came into view.

Lion leaped away from Charlie's grip and raced toward it, barking fiercely, his whole body shaking.

Charlie could make out the shapes of two men. He held his breath.

One of the men raised his arm and called out, "Looks like you've got a good watchdog there, Charlie Keller!"

It was Papa.

They woke Sadie so she could say good-bye.

"Lizzie is leaving, Sadie," Papa told her. "This is our friend Ed Dillon, who will help her get to Canada where she can be free."

"You're sure it's safe now?" Momma asked.

Papa nodded. "Yes, all the arrangements are made.

Besides, things are about to change in Kansas. The president of the United States has appointed a new governor named John Geary. He'll arrive soon, on September ninth. But already people are saying he'll be able to put an end to the fighting."

"We're hoping the proslavery folks will give up on Kansas. Eventually we'll pass some new, better laws," put in Ed Dillon. "You'll have your father back from now on, Charlie. And when I return your wagon I'll stay for a few days and help harvest your corn."

Lizzie held out her arms to Sadie. "I'll miss you, Sadie Sunshine."

"Thank you for everything, Lizzie," said Momma, handing her a bundle. "Here are some biscuits, and a dress I made for you."

Charlie wished he had something to give Lizzie. Then he remembered. He still had the little piece of type from the newspaper office. It wasn't much, but somehow it seemed just right.

He ran to find it and held it out to Lizzie. "It's a letter of type from a newspaper in Kansas, the *Kansas Free State*."

"Why, it's an 'L' for 'Lizzie,'" said Momma.

"Or for 'Liberty,'" suggested Papa.

Ida Jane smiled. "It's an 'L' to remind you of Lawrence."

Sadie wrapped her arms around Lizzie's legs and whispered, "It's for 'Love.'"

Lizzie smiled. She leaned down and hugged Sadie.

Lion came up and nudged Lizzie's hand.

Charlie grinned. "Lion doesn't want you to forget him, either. 'L' is for 'Lion.'"

Lizzie reached out and patted Lion gingerly on the head. "I never thought I'd like a dog. But I'll even miss you, Lion."

CHAPTER
TEN

Charlie spotted the doe before Lion did.

She was heading up a low hill, making her way through the tall grass. The September sun glinted off her sides. If she hadn't moved, Charlie might not have seen her at all.

"Look, Lion," he said softly.

The doe must have been a half mile away, at least. *She couldn't have heard me*, Charlie thought. But as soon as he spoke, her head came up. She froze, listening hard.

Then with a strong, graceful leap she bounded. She looked incredibly light, as if she might fly.

Above the deer the sky was filled with swirls of clouds. The sun was just low enough to paint them a deep purple. *Like a prairie violet*, Charlie thought.

Charlie could hear crickets in the grass, humming and chirping. The wind blew in his ears, making a kind of music, too.

"It's so beautiful," Charlie whispered to Lion. "Let's just stay and watch a while."

Charlie knew he would have other afternoons on the prairie. Of course on some of them he would be in school.

Mrs. Engle had been talking about starting a school at her place this fall, now that things had settled down and most of the border ruffians had gone back to Missouri.

Sadie wasn't too happy about the idea of school. "What if something happens to my chickens when I'm gone?"

"You're too young for school yet anyway," Charlie had told her. "But when you do go, Lion will watch your chickens during the day."

Ida Jane, though, couldn't wait for school to start.

"I can be a teacher myself when I'm fifteen," she had announced. "And that's exactly what I aim to do. And by then Kansas will be a free state!"

Of course, no one knew yet whether Kansas would enter the Union as a free state or not. But the Keller family would keep fighting against slavery. Papa was even talking to some folks in Lawrence to see if they could help in the Underground Railroad.

"Who knows?" he said. "Maybe Spring Creek will be a stop on the Liberty Line someday."

Momma nodded. "With the brave children we have, I believe we *could* be of help."

Charlie thought of Lizzie. He thought of everything that had happened since the first day Papa had told them about moving to Kansas. "Yes, let's help, Papa. Let's do what we can."

I'll have hundreds and hundreds of afternoons like this, because it's for sure now. We're here to stay, Charlie thought.

But this one afternoon seemed so perfect he wanted to remember it. He would write to Grandpa and tell him exactly what it felt like to stand under these prairie skies.

Charlie and Lion stood still. They stood until the deer was out of sight, and the sun sank.

"Time to go," Charlie said at last, his hand on Lion's fur. "It's time to go home."

BAKING-POWDER
✳BISCUITS✳

Charlie's mother bakes baking-powder biscuits in this story. Making biscuits was an everyday event on a farm at the time *Our Kansas Home* is set. In an article in the collection of the Kansas State Historical Society called "Daily Routine of a Kansas Farm Wife in the Last Quarter of the Nineteenth Century," Mrs. Georgie Steifer describes daily farm life based on her memories of her grandmother. She writes that in the morning women usually made a big batch of biscuits, which would then be eaten throughout the day. Biscuits were popular because they could be made more quickly than bread. This was especially helpful in the days before people could run to a store to get a loaf of bread.

There are many different recipes for baking-powder biscuits. Here is the one my parents (especially my dad!) always made at my house when I was a girl:

RUSS HOPKINSON'S BAKING-POWDER BISCUITS

2 cups flour

3 teaspoons baking powder

¼ teaspoon salt

1 tablespoon sugar

¼ cup Crisco (butter or margarine
may also be used)

1 cup milk

Combine ingredients quickly in a bowl. Spoon batter into an ungreased muffin tin, dividing equally among the cups. The batter will rise when baking, so don't fill the cups to the top. Bake at 450 degrees for about 12 minutes, or until golden brown. Makes twelve biscuits. Serve with butter and jam, or as strawberry shortcake.

ABOUT
OUR KANSAS HOME

Our Kansas Home is fiction, but it is based on a period of time in the 1850s when the Kansas Territory was known as "Bleeding Kansas." During this time people in our country were arguing about whether slavery should spread to new territories in the West. The summer of 1856, when this story takes place, was a time of conflict between proslavery people and free-state settlers in Kansas. Eventually Kansas entered the Union as a free state in 1861. Many historians think that studying what happened in Kansas helps us to better understand the roots of the Civil War.

In this book Charlie and his family and friends are made-up. Other characters that are mentioned, such as Sheriff Samuel Jones, John Brown, and Charles Robinson, really lived. Some events in the story, such as the burning of the Free State Hotel in Lawrence on May 21, 1856, are based on things that did take place.

To research the Prairie Skies books I read many works written by people who lived in Kansas during this time. For instance, many abolitionists lived in Lawrence,

Kansas, and the town played an active role in the Underground Railroad. The story of Lizzie is based on an incident in Richard Cordley's *Pioneer Days in Kansas*, written in 1903. Mr. Cordley and his wife were living in a stone house south of Lawrence in 1859 when a young woman named Lizzie, who was fleeing slavery, came to stay with them until arrangements could be made to take her to Canada on the Underground Railroad.

When they learned Lizzie's master was pursuing her, the Cordleys came up with a plan to hide her. Mrs. Cordley's friend would lie in bed, pretending to be sick, with Mrs. Cordley at her side. Lizzie would then hide between the mattress and the feather bed. They felt sure the searchers would not disturb a sick woman. Mr. Cordley wrote that Lizzie said, "I will make myself just as small as ever I can, and I will lie as still as still can be." Eventually Lizzie was helped to go to Canada by her friends in Lawrence.

History is like a giant quilt, with many pieces. *Our Kansas Home* tells only a small part of a complicated story. You can learn more about Kansas history by reading other books, visiting museums or historical sites, or looking on the Internet.

More information on Kansas history can be found at:

Kansas State Historical Society
www.kshs.org

The Kansas Collection
www.kancoll.org

Ready-for-Chapters

Enjoy the very best first chapter book fiction in Ready-for-Chapters books from Aladdin Paperbacks.

❏ **Jake Drake, Bully Buster**
by Andrew Clements

❏ **Annabel the Actress Starring in Gorilla My Dreams**
by Ellen Conford

❏ **The Bears on Hemlock Mountain**
by Alice Dalgliesh

❏ **The Courage of Sarah Noble**
by Alice Dalgliesh

❏ **The Girl with 500 Middle Names**
by Margaret Peterson Haddix

❏ **The Werewolf Club**
#1 The Magic Pretzel
by Daniel Pinkwater

❏ **The Werewolf Club**
#2 The Lunchroom of Doom
by Daniel Pinkwater

❏ **The Werewolf Club**
#3 The Werewolf Club Meets Dorkula
by Daniel Pinkwater

❏ **The Cobble Street Cousins**
#1 In Aunt Lucy's Kitchen
by Cynthia Rylant

❏ **The Cobble Street Cousins**
#2 A Little Shopping
by Cynthia Rylant

❏ **The Cobble Street Cousins**
#3 Special Gifts
by Cynthia Rylant

❏ **Third-Grade Detectives**
#1 The Clue of the Left-Handed Envelope
by George Edward Stanley

❏ **Third-Grade Detectives**
#2 The Puzzle of the Pretty Pink Handkerchief
by George Edward Stanley

❏ **Third-Grade Detectives**
#3 The Mystery of the Hairy Tomatoes
by George Edward Stanley

Aladdin Paperbacks

Simon & Schuster Children's Publishing • www.SimonSaysKids.com